WIDE WORLD

PEOPLE *of the*
POLAR REGIONS

Jen Green

RSVP
RAINTREE
STECK-VAUGHN
PUBLISHERS
The Steck-Vaughn Company

Austin, Texas

WIDE WORLD

PEOPLE *of the* **GRASSLANDS**
PEOPLE *of the* **DESERTS**
PEOPLE *of the* **ISLANDS**

PEOPLE *of the* **MOUNTAINS**
PEOPLE *of the* **POLAR REGIONS**
PEOPLE *of the* **RAIN FORESTS**

Cover: An Inuit man in the Canadian Northwest Territories looking for caribou from a snowmobile

Title page: A Chukchi herder from Siberia

This page and Contents page: An Inuit village by the sea in Greenland

Published by Raintree Steck-Vaughn Publishers, an imprint of Steck-Vaughn Company

Library of Congress Cataloging-in-Publication Data
Green, Jen.
People of the polar regions / Jen Green.
    p.   cm.—(Wide world)
    Includes bibliographical references and index.
    Summary: Describes the history of the polar peoples, how they live and work, and the seasons and geographic features of the lands of the midnight sun.
    ISBN 0-8172-5065-4
    1. Arctic peoples—Juvenile literature.
    2. Arctic regions—Juvenile literature.
    3. Human ecology—Arctic regions—Juvenile literature.
    [1. Arctic peoples. 2. Arctic regions. 3. Human ecology.
    4. Ecology.]
    I. Title. II. Series.
    GN673.G74   1998
    304.2'0911—dc21   97-38625

Printed in Italy. Bound in the United States.
1 2 3 4 5 6 7 8 9 0 03 02 01 00 99

Contents

Surviving the Cold

The polar regions are the coldest, most hostile places on earth. Out on the polar plateau in the howling wind, skin exposed to the air begins to freeze in minutes. Plastic shrinks, and hot drinks cool and freeze over while people are still drinking them.

Arctic peoples

Despite these harsh conditions, people have lived in the Arctic, the lands of the far north, for thousands of years. The Saami of Scandinavia and the peoples of northern Russia lived by herding reindeer. The Inuit from Greenland and the far north of North America survived by hunting. One of the first Europeans to meet the Inuit wrote: "Those beasts, fishes, and birds which they kill are their meat, drink, clothing, houses, bedding, shoes—and almost all their riches." Today, many Arctic peoples live very much like people in other parts of Europe and North America. But they also take pride in their traditional skills.

An Inuit boy with his father. ▶
The word "Inuit" simply means
"the people."

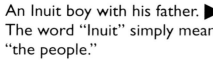

Undiscovered country

Antarctica, at the opposite end of the earth, has never been inhabited. In fact, this vast continent was totally unknown only 200 years ago, and many inland areas have still not been explored. Scientists from many nations live at research bases in Antarctica. Most visit in the summer to study the weather, land, and wildlife. At the research base at the South Pole, the flags of many nations fly. They symbolize the concern of people all around the world to preserve this frozen wilderness.

▲ Huge icebergs are lashed by waves in the stormy Antarctic seas.

Polar Legends
Before Europeans visited the polar regions, there were many myths and legends about these unknown lands. Antarctica was thought to be a vast, frozen land guarded by ghosts, dragons, and sea-monsters that would destroy all ships that sailed too near.

Frozen Lands

The Arctic and Antarctic have the harshest climates in the world. During the Arctic summer, the temperature rarely rises above 50° F (10° C). In winter, it often drops to -40° F (-40° C) at night. Antarctica is even colder.

Lands of the midnight sun

The earth is tilted on its axis, so as the earth moves around the sun, one pole leans toward the sun and the other is tilted away. Both polar regions have a time in summer when the sun never sets and a period in winter when it never rises.

▼ The midnight sun on Svalbard in the Arctic. At midsummer the sun never sets.

Continuous Darkness
Scientists who spend the whole winter at research bases near the poles do not see the sun for over two months. The continuous darkness sometimes makes people tense or depressed. In 1983, a scientist in Antarctica burned down his research base so that he would not have to spend the winter there!

The Arctic

Although the Arctic and the Antarctic are both cold places, there are many differences between the two. The Arctic is an icy ocean surrounded by the continents of North America, Europe, and Asia. The shallow Arctic seas are covered with drifting floes—ice sheets up to 7 ft. (2 m) thick. Greenland, the world's largest island, lies in the Arctic, and most of it is covered with a permanent ice cap. The other lands inside the Arctic Circle are mostly tundra—treeless lowlands that are covered with snow in winter.

The North Pole in the ▶ Arctic is the most northerly point on Earth.

▲ Ice floes and icebergs like this one drift in the Arctic Ocean.

☐ Sea ice

The Arctic

Alaska (U.S.)

Siberia

Arctic Circle

R U S S I A

CANADA

ARCTIC OCEAN

+ North Pole

Novaya Zemla

G R E E N L A N D

Svalbard

N O R W A Y

FINLAND

SWEDEN

7

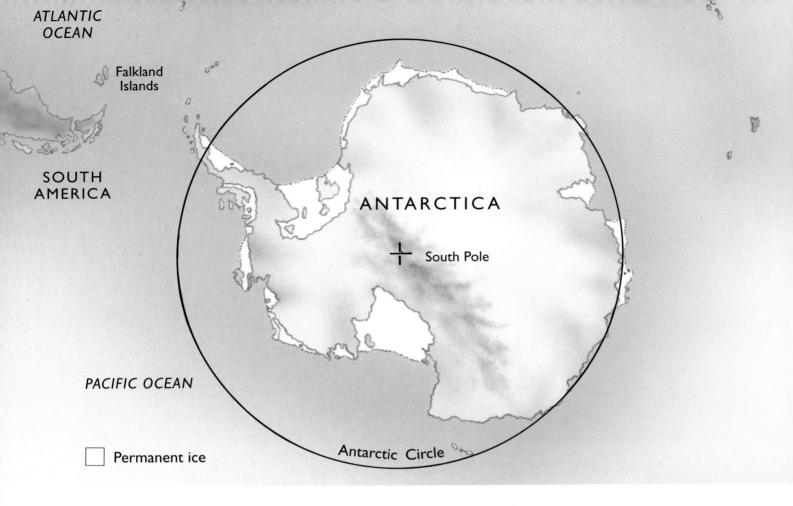

ATLANTIC
OCEAN

Falkland
Islands

SOUTH
AMERICA

ANTARCTICA

South Pole

PACIFIC OCEAN

Antarctic Circle

Permanent ice

▲ Scientists now think that
Antarctica is not a single giant
mass of land. The western area
is made up of islands, joined by
ice, known as the Antarctic
Peninsula.

Antarctica

Antarctica is very different from the Arctic. It is a huge
continent, larger than Australia or the United States,
surrounded by icy waters. The ice that covers the land is
over 2.5 mi. (4 km) thick in some places. The lowest
temperature ever recorded, -128° F (-89° C), was
measured there. It is also one of the windiest places on
earth—an early explorer nicknamed it the "Kingdom of
Blizzards." The howling winds make the temperatures
feel even colder.

Weather and climate

The polar regions have brief summers and long,
freezing winters, which last for eight or nine months. In
summer, the Arctic is still cold, because the sun is too
low in the sky to give much warmth. But in the long
daylight hours, the snow melts from the tundra,
flowers bloom, and the air is filled with buzzing insects.

Even in midsummer, Antarctica is too cold for the ice on land to melt. Temperatures in the sea are warmer than on land, so much of the sea ice melts. Seen from outer space, this icy continent appears to shrink each year in summer and grow bigger again in winter when the sea freezes over.

▼ Icebergs, like this one off Greenland, break off from glaciers or ice sheets on land. Then they are carried out to sea.

Snow and Ice

As winter begins, temperatures drop and ice forms in the polar oceans. At first, a thin layer of ice forms over the surface of the sea. Wind and waves break this layer into slabs of ice called "pancake ice." The ice then thickens to become "pack ice." On land, all ice is formed of compacted snow—snow pressed down by its own weight. Although it does not snow much at the poles, the snow keeps building up in layers, to form a thick crust.

Animal life

A much wider range of animals is found in the far north than in the far south. On land, Arctic animals include polar bears, Arctic hares and foxes, and large, shaggy cattle called musk oxen. All these animals have thick fur or hairy coats to keep out the cold. The Arctic seas are also rich in wildlife, including seals, walruses, and whales. For thousands of years, the peoples of the Arctic have hunted these animals for food and for their skins, which they use to make warm clothing.

The continent of Antarctica is too cold for animals to survive on land, except for a few tiny insects and spiders. But the waters surrounding Antarctica teem with life. Tiny shrimp called krill are eaten by fish, seals, penguins, and whales. The blue whale, which is the largest animal on earth, lives in these waters.

▼ An Inuit hunter skins a seal that he has caught in a net under the ice.

Mineral resources

Metals such as tin, iron, lead, and zinc are found in the Arctic. Vast amounts of oil and natural gas have been found in Canada, Alaska, and Siberia. Coal is mined in Alaska, in Siberia, and on the island of Svalbard. Antarctica also has minerals buried under the ice cap, but, to protect the environment, no mining is allowed there.

Reindeer

Reindeer (or caribou, as they are known in North America) are important Arctic animals. Vast herds of reindeer roam the tundra. For hundreds of years, the Saami of Lapland and the people of northern Russia traveled with the herds. They depended on the reindeer for meat and to pull sleds. Reindeer skins were made into clothing, and into tents for shelter. The antlers were used to make harpoons.

History of Polar Peoples

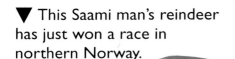

▼ This Saami man's reindeer has just won a race in northern Norway.

Unlike the animals of the Arctic, humans have no fur and little fat to keep them warm. Yet people have lived in the far north for thousands of years. No one visited the far south until the early nineteenth century.

The first Arctic people

Many thousands of years ago, the Yakut and the Chukchi peoples lived in Arctic Russia. These peoples were ancestors of the Samoyed people living in Russia today. They led a mostly nomadic life, herding reindeer and hunting. In Scandinavia, the Saami people also traveled the tundra and the forests, following the reindeer.

Ancestors of the Inuit

About 8,000 years ago, Asian people from Mongolia migrated eastward into North America. Some settled in the Arctic, to become the ancestors of modern Inuit people. Over 1,000 years ago, a group called the Thule became the most important group in the area. Instead of traveling constantly from place to place to hunt, as earlier peoples had done, the Thule built houses. These had stone walls dug partly into the ground and had roofs of turf and stone. The rafters were made of whalebone.

This map shows the main ▶ groups of people who live in the Arctic today.

The Thule survived by hunting polar animals for meat, which they ate raw. During the long winters, they speared seals that came up through holes in the ice to breathe. When the ice began to melt, they hunted seals and fish in kayaks, canoes made of sealskin stretched over a framework of wood or bone. To hunt large bowhead whales, teams of men would set off in larger boats called *umiaks*. When traveling on land, they harnessed wooden sleds to teams of husky dogs that pulled them along.

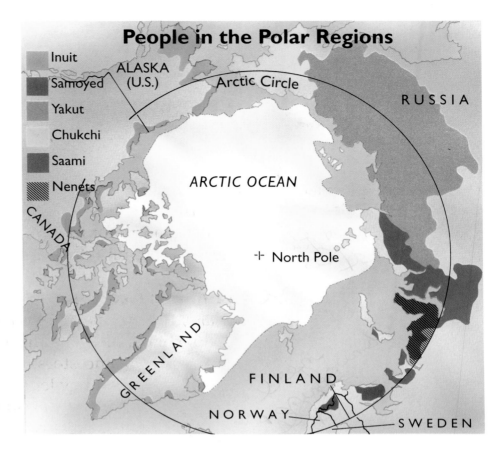

People in the Polar Regions

Inuit
Samoyed
Yakut
Chukchi
Saami
Nenets

ALASKA (U.S.)
Arctic Circle
RUSSIA

CANADA

ARCTIC OCEAN

⊹ North Pole

GREENLAND

FINLAND

NORWAY

SWEDEN

▼ Igloos like this one are the traditional shelters used by the Inuit on hunting trips. Igloos are made of blocks of ice.

A nineteenth-century ▶ painting showing hunters catching a whale. Oil from whales was used as fuel for lamps and was made into soap.

Europeans in the Arctic

Using their traditional skills, the Inuit survived in the Arctic for thousands of years. Until a few hundred years ago, they had little contact with Europeans. But in the 1600s, European sailors began to explore Arctic waters. Soon, hunting ships were arriving every spring to slaughter seals and whales.

Trading furs

During the 1700s, Russian explorers crossed the Bering Straits to reach Alaska. Russian merchants began to trade with Inuit trappers and the Aleut, a coastal people related to the Inuit. In northern Canada, merchants from Europe set up trading posts. Here, Inuit trappers exchanged the fur of animals, such as foxes and otters, for rifles, knives, and tools. The Hudson Bay Company, set up in 1821, soon controlled the trade in furs.

◀ This picture of an Inuit woman and her child was drawn by a European explorer who visited the Arctic in the late 1500s.

Changing lives

By the 1800s, many Inuit depended on the traders for their living. Vast areas of land, and the lives of the Inuit who lived there, were controlled by a few companies. Some Inuit even became slaves. Europeans introduced the Inuit to new foods such as sugar and alcohol and tobacco. They brought diseases such as measles and tuberculosis to the Inuit camps. These diseases had been unknown in the Arctic, and thousands of Inuit died because they had no natural resistance to them.

Lessons from the Inuit

The first explorers to reach the North and South Poles were helped by the Inuit or used Inuit methods of survival. The American explorer Robert Peary reached the North Pole in 1909 with the help of Inuit teams, who mostly led the way. The Norwegian Roald Amundsen was first to the South Pole, in 1912. His team wore Inuit-style clothing and used huskies to haul their supplies.

This engraving shows ▶ Roald Amundsen and his team struggling across Antarctica to reach the South Pole between 1911 and 1912. The engraving was made just after the expedition.

Opening up the Arctic

In the 1880s, gold was discovered at the Yukon River in Alaska. Thousands of prospectors arrived to make their fortunes, and many new settlements grew up. The traditional Inuit way of life continued to change. During the Cold War, the United States set up a line of early warning stations across the Arctic, in case of an attack from the USSR. These stations provided work for the Inuit, and more settlements grew.

New industries

In 1968, vast areas of oil and gas were discovered at Prudhoe Bay in Alaska. New roads and railroads had to be made to reach the drilling sites, and pipelines were built to transport the oil and gas. But the Inuit people, who had lived in these lands for centuries, began to demand a say in what was done.

▼ Prospectors mining for gold in Alaska, around 1900

Exploring Antarctica

Two hundred years ago, Antarctica had not been discovered. Between 1773 and 1775, the explorer Captain James Cook sailed around Antarctica without seeing land, but he did report seeing huge numbers of whales and seals in the surrounding ocean. His story brought other sailors to the area to hunt. It was these sailors who first sighted land, in the 1820s.

Between 1830 and 1850, the coast of Antarctica was explored by ships from France, Russia, Great Britain, and the United States. As these expeditions mapped the coastline, each claimed some of the land for its own country. By 1900, Antarctica had been divided up among nations like a big pie. But in 1959, twelve countries came together to sign the Antarctic Treaty. They agreed to suspend their claims to land in Antarctica. They also decided that the continent should be used only for peaceful purposes, such as scientific research.

▲ Scientists setting up their equipment in Antarctica

Work in the Polar Regions

In the Arctic today, only a few people still do traditional work, such as herding reindeer. Many work in industries that use the natural resources of the region, such as mining. Some Inuit have their own businesses, running fish-processing plants or small craft factories.

Seal-hunting

During the 1960s and 1970s, seal hunting was a major industry. Hundreds of thousands of seals were killed for their fur, because fur coats were very fashionable in Europe and North America. But by the 1980s, most people had started to think that killing animals for fashion was wrong. The seal industry collapsed, leaving many Inuit hunters without work. Now, seal hunting still goes on, but on a much smaller scale.

▼ An Inuit man hunts seals. Most hunters today use binoculars and rifles with telescopic sights, rather than harpoons.

Fishing

Fishing is big business in the polar regions. Fleets from Europe, North America, and Japan fish the Arctic seas for cod, haddock, and prawns. Salmon are farmed in rivers. Fish and krill are caught in the Antarctic. So many fish have been caught that some are in danger of being wiped out. There are now strict rules about the kinds of nets that can be used and the quantity of fish that each nation can catch. Large-scale whaling is banned, although some Arctic peoples are allowed to catch a small number of whales each year.

▲ A Norwegian trawler fishes for prawns in the Arctic Ocean.

Herders

Reindeer herding was the traditional work of the Saami and the peoples of Arctic Russia. But nowadays only a few Saami herd reindeer. Those who do use snowmobiles or helicopters to find and drive their animals. Many Saami now work in farms or offices or in the forestry industry.

▼ A Chukchi reindeer herder in Siberia. The life is hard, but there is a great sense of freedom out on the tundra.

Herders Today

There are about 35,000 Saami today, living in Norway, Sweden, Finland, and Russia. Only about 10 percent of them are reindeer herders.

Drilling for gas and oil

Since oil and natural gas were discovered at Prudhoe Bay in Alaska in 1968, drilling for these natural resources has become the state's most important industry. As the seas are frozen for most of the year, it is difficult to transport the oil by ship. Between 1974 and 1977, the Trans-Alaska Pipeline was built. It carries the oil from Prudhoe Bay across Alaska to Valdez, a port that does not freeze in winter. From there, the oil is shipped south in giant tankers.

▼ An offshore rig in the frozen waters of Prudhoe Bay, Alaska

Many jobs

The oil and gas industries provide work for many people in the Arctic. More than 6,000 people now work at Prudhoe Bay. The towns and settlements that have sprung up in the area provide work for store clerks, clerical workers, and technicians. But not all the work is permanent. For example, hundreds of construction workers are needed to build oil rigs and pipelines. But when these are completed, the people who built them may lose their jobs.

Working in the polar regions can be very difficult. Workers on oil rigs are cut off from their families for months at a time. In Arctic Russia and elsewhere, workers mining gold and other minerals may have to work knee-deep in icy, swirling water.

Drilling in the Arctic
The cold conditions, snow, and high winds in the Arctic cause problems for the oil industry. Giant icebergs and blizzards threaten oil rigs at sea. In the Arctic Ocean, oil is drilled from artificial islands and drilling ships that can be moved out of the way of drifting ice.

Damaged lands

The companies that run the oil, gas, and mining industries make a lot of money. The countries that own the land make a lot of money, too. But these industries can damage the landscape and cause pollution. On the island of Svalbard, coal mines scar the landscape and affect local wildlife such as seals and seabirds. In Siberia, the Nenets people have lost many of their traditional reindeer pastures because the oil and gas industries have developed there.

▼ The Trans-Alaska Pipeline cuts through traditional Inuit hunting grounds. In places, it is raised up so that caribou can pass under it.

An oil worker at ▶ Prudhoe Bay in Alaska. He is wearing thick clothes for protection against the bitter cold.

21

Science at the poles

Many scientists work at research bases in the polar regions. Studies of conditions in the Antarctic are especially important, because there are no mines or factories there to pollute the natural world.

These scientists in ▶ Antarctica are removing samples of ice. By counting the layers in the ice, they can find out how old it is.

Polar ice is made up of snow that has built up in layers year after year. Scientists can drill down and remove samples of ice that formed thousands of years ago. They analyze the samples to find out how much pollution was in the atmosphere when the snow fell. Scientists also study the weather, rocks and soil, and polar plants and animals. Recently, they have discovered that the blood of tiny polar animals, such as mites, contains a kind of natural antifreeze that keeps them alive in very cold weather.

▲ A tourist photographs an Emperor penguin chick in Antarctica.

Tourism

Tourism is a growing industry in the Arctic and Antarctic. When the sea ice melts, cruise ships bring tourists to look at the landscape and to photograph seals, whales, and birds. Some people fear that tourist trips disturb the animals during their vital breeding seasons. But tour operators use experienced local guides who know a lot about the land and wildlife. Visitors learn more about the natural world and the importance of protecting it. Tourism also provides jobs for many local people. They work as tour guides, boat operators, souvenir sellers, and restaurant staff.

Homes and Buildings

Most people in the Arctic live in snug modern houses or apartments with indoor plumbing and electricity. Many have central heating, television, and VCRs. But there are a few people who still live in traditional homes. Out on the tundra, the Saami and, in particular, the Siberian reindeer herders live in tents. Their homes are made of reindeer or walrus skin, stretched over a framework of poles. The floor is a layer of branches covered with animal skins. A hole in the top of the tent lets smoke escape from the cooking fire.

▼ These tents are made of reindeer skins. They belong to Nenets herders in Siberia.

Arctic capital

The Arctic today has many modern settlements, including bustling ports and industrial towns that have grown up around mining areas. Nuuk in Greenland is the world's most northerly capital. Nuuk's buildings and the daily lives of its people are similar to those in any European town. Only Inuit clothes flapping on a clothesline or a package of seal meat hanging from a balcony show that this is Greenland.

An Inuit settlement

Igloolik is a small Inuit settlement on the shores of the Foxe Basin, in the far north of Canada. Today, it is home to about 1,000 people. There are few natural building materials nearby, so prefabricated houses have been carried in by ship. Water is brought in by truck each week, and sewage is removed. The village has a library, a community hall, two churches, and a school. The two stores are well stocked with groceries. Sports facilities include a swimming pool and an ice-hockey rink.

▲ Igloolik, like many Inuit settlements today, has modern buildings and power cables overhead.

Antarctic town

McMurdo, nicknamed "Mactown," is a U.S. scientific base in Antarctica. This tiny town is made up of laboratories, workshops, and dormitories. It also has a chapel, a large mess hall where people eat and drink, and a gym hut near the helicopter pad. During the summer months, McMurdo is a place where scientists can work and relax. But in the driving snow of a fierce winter blizzard, all landmarks disappear. Outside, people have to feel their way around, using ropes slung between the buildings.

Scientist's Home

Vanda is a small research base out on the Antarctic plateau, where four scientists from New Zealand live and work. Solar panels provide electricity for the radio and the fire alarm. There are lights, but they are never used in summer because it is light all the time. The scientists chip blocks of ice from a nearby lake to melt for drinking water. The toilet is a three-sided shack 328 ft. (100 m) away, without a door!

▼ McMurdo is the largest settlement in the Antarctic.

Building problems

Ice and snow cause special building problems in the polar regions. When the foundations of buildings are dug into frozen soil, the permafrost may melt, causing the buildings to lean crookedly or to sink. To solve this problem, some buildings are perched on special metal frames. A similar problem affects electricity and telephone poles. In Igloolik and other Arctic settlements, these are set into concrete bases, not into the ground.

Out on the ice cap in Greenland or Antarctica, snow does not melt but builds up year by year. A hut built on the ice may disappear beneath the snow within five years. Some huts are now built inside corrugated steel tubes that are reinforced to bear the weight of the snow. Tunnels, ventilation shafts, and chimneys have to be extended every year to reach the surface.

▲ The Amundsen–Scott research base at the South Pole

▼ This new building near the South Pole has been built on a metal frame so that it can be raised above the snow level each year.

Transportation and Communications

In the Arctic, Inuit people traditionally used a *komatik*, or wooden sled, hauled by huskies for transportation. Today, the sleds are more likely to be pulled by snowmobiles, small gasoline-driven vehicles that carry one or two passengers and can pull heavy loads. Snowmobiles can travel faster than walking pace over snowy roads or rough country with steep slopes.

Husky or snowmobile?

Some Inuit hunters prefer to travel with huskies, while others use snowmobiles. There are good arguments for each. "When you're out hunting, machines don't bark and chase the caribou away," claims a European survival expert. "Machines break down, dogs will always get you back. And you can't eat your snowmobile," replies one Inuit hunter.

This snowmobile has skis at ▶ the front and caterpillar tracks behind. The tracks give a good grip on snow and ice.

Traveling across the ice

Larger vehicles are also used in the Arctic and Antarctic. Modified tractors are often used to cross rough country where jagged ice ridges, called *sastrugi,* are created by the wind. Sno-cats have high cabins set on caterpillar tracks. Scientists or tourists crossing the ice cap might travel in a "train," a line of heated carriages pulled by a powerful engine. The carriages can include sleeping and eating areas, but they give a noisy, bumpy ride and sometimes cause motion sickness.

▲ Learning to control a team of huskies like this takes much skill and practice.

▼ A tundra buggy carrying tourists in the Arctic. Even sturdy vehicles like this can be difficult to drive in blizzards.

▲ An Inuit hunter sitting in a traditional kayak adjusts his harpoon line.

On the water

Until recent times, when the sea ice melted in the summer, Inuit people took to the water in *kayaks* and *umiaks*, larger boats rowed by hunters. Teams of men would haul the boats over the ice to the water's edge. These days, boats are more likely to be towed to the water by snowmobiles, and on fishing trips and whale hunts, boats are gasoline-driven.

Danger at sea

Polar waters hold many dangers. Sea ice is one hazard. If the sea freezes over or pack ice closes around a ship, it will be trapped. Icebergs, huge chunks of floating ice that can be as big as islands, are also a menace, especially in fog or darkness. The most famous sea disaster, the loss of the ocean liner *Titanic*, was caused by an iceberg. Launched in 1912, this luxury ship was thought to be unsinkable. But crossing the North Atlantic Ocean on its very first voyage, it struck a large iceberg. Water gushed through the hull, and the ship quickly sank, killing 1,513 of the 2,224 people on board.

Modern ships in polar waters are equipped with radar equipment to detect icebergs and pack ice. Ships' radios warn of approaching storms. Planes, helicopters, and satellites help sailors find areas of open water in sea ice. But accidents still happen. In 1989, the Russian cruiser *Maxim Gorky*, sailing off Iceland, hit pack ice in thick fog. The passengers escaped onto the ice and were rescued by boat and helicopter before the ship sank.

▼ Icebreakers like this one are used to clear routes for other ships to use. The bows are reinforced with steel plates so they can cut through the ice.

▲ A small aircraft brings supplies to a village in Greenland. Husky teams are used to carry the supplies from the landing strip.

Air travel

The ideal way to travel in the polar regions is by air. Airplanes and helicopters transport equipment and passengers across the vast distances of the tundra and the ice cap. Air travel is part of everyday life, and people travel to meetings or to visit friends by plane.

The polar weather can be a problem for aircraft. One journalist described the scene inside a plane during a blizzard in Antarctica: "The pounding seemed endless —a rolling, jolting tumble, slamming the passengers… against the walls. The plane could have been going end over end, falling right off the earth."

The "bad weather zone," where snowstorms and high winds are worst, is at ground level or just above it. This can make takeoff and landing very dangerous. In "white-out" conditions, when light reflecting off clouds and snow makes the sky and ground appear to merge, pilots may be unable to see the ground to land safely. Ice can affect the plane's navigation systems too, so the pilot is truly "flying blind."

Aerial Explorers

Today, most exploration of the polar regions is carried out by air. Planes fly over remote areas that have never been reached by land, to map mountains, glaciers, and high plateaus. In 1946–1947, the U.S. carried out a huge program of air exploration called Operation High Jump. It charted many new islands and mountain ranges.

Telecommunications

Communications systems are vital in the frozen wastes of the Arctic and Antarctic. In isolated settlements, people can keep in touch with the outside world by radio and satellite telephone, even in poor weather. Hunters and trappers can contact their base, using high-frequency radio. In lonely areas, people can turn on the television to watch programs broadcast via satellite links. The Arctic is now part of a world that seems to be shrinking rapidly, thanks to modern technology.

▼ This Inuit man is using his radio to contact Igloolik from his camp out on the ice.

Daily Life and Leisure

The cold is part of everyday life in the Arctic and Antarctic. The Inuit, Saami, and Siberian peoples have always been expert at making warm clothing from animal skins. Traditional Inuit clothes consist of two layers: an outer layer with the fur turned outward against the weather, and an inner layer with the fur next to the skin. The animal skins used to be sewn together with reindeer sinew. Now, many Inuit use dental floss as thread.

Today, most people wear modern clothes made of synthetic materials. They wear many lightweight layers rather than heavy skins. A variety of fabrics can be used to keep the wearer warm or dry, to carry sweat away, or to keep out the wind. An Inuit hunter might wear jeans and a sweater with a traditional fur anorak (an Inuit word) and *mukluks*—deerskin boots. Many Inuit teenagers wear Western-style sports clothes.

▼ These young Inuit girls are wearing warm, Western-style clothing to keep out the cold.

▲ Saami reindeer herders cook fish over the fire in their tent. Many Arctic people still eat mainly local meat and fish.

Food

A few hundred years ago, the diet of Arctic people was almost entirely meat. In the summer, berries, fish, and birds' eggs added variety. Reindeer and seal meat, including the fatty blubber, contain all the vitamins and minerals they needed for good health.

A wider range of food is now available, including fruit and vegetables, but having a more varied diet has not always made people healthier than they were before. Tobacco, alcohol, and sugary foods have damaged some people's health. Packaged foods and other groceries are also very expensive because the cost of transporting them from the south is added to the price.

Sports and recreation

In their free time, the people of the Arctic enjoy themselves in many ways. Sports connected with the snow and ice are popular. Skiing is thought to have been invented by the Saami people. Many villages and towns have ice rinks where people can skate or play curling and ice hockey. Sometimes the icy streets are also used for practice.

Old and new

Many Arctic schools and villages have gyms, where traditional sports are played along with modern games. Swimming and basketball are very popular in Inuit communities, as well as games such as high kicking and arm wrestling. In some areas, competitions are held to test skills such as seal skinning. Inuit hunters race their husky teams, and reindeer races are popular among Saami people.

The Vanda Swimming Club

Vanda Research Base in Antarctica has an unusual tradition. Newcomers and visitors are invited to join the Vanda Swimming Club. But to become members, they must plunge into the freezing waters of Lake Vanda, through a hole hacked into the ice!

▼ A traditional Saami wedding in northern Norway. The bride's shawl is covered with brooches.

▼ Blanket tossing is a traditional Inuit sport.

▲ An Inuit teenager and his grandfather looking for caribou in Alaska. Some schools arrange their term times so that pupils can go with older relatives to learn how to hunt.

Schools

Education has brought many benefits to the peoples of the Arctic, but it has brought some disadvantages, too. Governments far away in the south decide what Arctic children should learn in school. So lessons have often been about subjects such as farming and life in city suburbs, not about the Arctic. Until recently, all lessons were in English, Russian, Danish, or another European language, instead of the local Arctic languages.

Lately some of this has changed. Children in Arctic Russia and Scandinavia used to be sent away to study in schools and colleges far from home. Now the boarding-school system is being abandoned or improved. More schools, especially primary schools, are teaching children in their own local languages. Traditional skills such as sled making, trapping, and sewing are taught in many areas. "The most important thing is to teach our young people our way of life. Then they will be ready to face what comes," a village elder says.

Clash of cultures

Daily life in the Arctic is a lot easier now than it was a hundred years ago. People live in comfortable homes and shop in supermarkets instead of spending hours each day hunting in the cold. But modern life is more complicated, too. Everyone now needs regular jobs to earn the money for food, equipment, or gas for snowmobiles. Yet a great many people, particularly the young, are out of work. Many Arctic people feel their identity is being swept away, as more and more of them have begun to speak European languages rather than the traditional languages of the Arctic regions.

An Inuit woman with a blanket ▶ made of bird feathers. Lately, people have taken a new pride in their history and in their traditional skills.

Development and Conservation

Eight nations own lands in the Arctic. Decisions about these lands are made by governments in capital cities far away. Industry and new developments have brought many changes and some problems for the local people.

Pollution

One of the main problems has been pollution. The oil and gas industries have been partly to blame for this. Drilling and new pipelines have damaged the land and disturbed wildlife. There have been some serious accidents, too. In 1989, the oil tanker *Exxon Valdez* ran aground in Alaska. Within hours, millions of gallons of oil had spilled into the sea. The cleanup operation took many months.

▼ A worker cleans up oil from the *Exxon Valdez*. The disaster killed fish stocks on which the local fishermen depended.

The *Exxon Valdez* oil spill:

- killed 1,000 sea otters
- destroyed up to 100,000 sea birds
- polluted 1,200 mi. (1,900 km) of coastline

Disaster at Chernobyl

In 1986, a nuclear reactor at the Chernobyl power station in the USSR caught fire. Explosions sent a cloud of radioactive gases high into the air. Radioactive pollution was brought down in the rain over a wide area, including the tundra in Scandinavia and Siberia. Lichen and grasses became contaminated, and then the reindeer that fed on the lichen became contaminated, too. Thousands had to be slaughtered, and this meant that many reindeer herders no longer had a way of earning a living.

Scientists have recently discovered that pollution can affect a wide area, not just the local region. Radiation from Chernobyl was measured in the Antarctic ice, on the other side of the world. Chemicals from industry and farming in developed countries find their way into the air, sea, and land of the polar regions, where they affect the local wildlife.

▲ Scientists have measured high levels of poisonous chemicals in polar bears. The polar bears have taken these in through their food.

▲ Spilled oil burns after a leak from a pipeline in Arctic Russia. Campaigners are trying to make sure such accidents cannot happen in the future.

New plans

The oil, gas, and mining companies have plans for new developments in the Arctic. When the oil fields were opened at Prudhoe Bay in Alaska, the United States government created a large nature preserve nearby to protect the local wildlife. Now, the oil companies want to drill there, too. In Canada and Scandinavia, there are plans to dam rivers to generate hydroelectricity. Hydroelectric power does not cause pollution. But when rivers are dammed, whole areas of land get flooded.

People power

The people of the Arctic have started to oppose new hydroelectric projects and mining plans. In Norway in 1979, the Saami fought a plan to dam the Alta River. The dam would have flooded reindeer pastures and affected salmon streams. After two years, when 20,000 people had joined the protest, the Norwegian government dropped the plan. In Canada and the United States, the Inuit and other Arctic groups have opposed the building of new dams and the transportation of oil by pipeline or by icebreaker. Both of these, they say, damage the natural world. If there were an accident, such as another oil spill, it would cause terrible pollution.

New treaty

In 1990, the nations that signed the Antarctic Treaty in 1959 (see page 17) met again. They signed a new agreement, called the Protocol to the Antarctic Treaty, which strengthened the old treaty and added new rules to protect wildlife. They decided to ban all mining in Antarctica, and they set up guidelines to guard against pollution.

Whaling in Antarctica

Whaling began in Antarctica in 1904. By the 1970s, many whale species were threatened with extinction. In 1987, all the nations that fished in Antarctica agreed to stop commercial whaling. They have also agreed to limit fishing.

▼ New efforts are being made to protect the beautiful icy wilderness of Antarctica.

The Future

Today, many different organizations campaign in the polar regions. International protest groups, such as Greenpeace, have helped stop commercial whaling. All over the Arctic, local people are forming their own political groups. They demand that governments recognize their rights in areas where their people have lived for centuries. They want a say in how these lands are run.

Arctic Peoples United

In 1977, the Inuit Circumpolar Conference brought Inuit and other Arctic peoples together for the first time. This group now works to make sure local people are involved in any plans for new developments in the Arctic. In 1983, the organization was recognized by the United Nations.

"Our land"

Inuit groups have been very effective in gaining better rights. In 1979, Greenland was granted home rule. This meant that the people could make many of their own laws, although their territory remained part of Denmark. In northern Canada and Alaska, Arctic people are claiming lands where their people have lived for generations. In northern Canada, the Inuit have gained an area about the size of Norway. They call it Nunavut, which means "our land."

◄ These Inuit children hope to have a say in what happens to their lands in the future.

New hope

Many wildlife preserves have been set up in the polar regions.
Northeast Greenland has become one of the world's largest
wildlife preserves. In 1994, Antarctica became a sanctuary for
whales. The Inuit, Saami, and other Arctic peoples are trying
to use the good things from the developed world, while
holding onto their own cultures. Many believe that education
holds the key to the future. Some young people train as
lawyers, teachers, and scientists. They will help make sure the
polar regions are protected for years to come.

▲ A hunter and his
traditional husky team
rest in front of a
modern satellite dish.

Glossary

Arctic Circle An imaginary line around the earth. All the lands north of this line have at least one day a year when the sun never sets.

Axis An imaginary line through the center of the earth, between the North and South poles.

Blubber A layer of fat that keeps animals such as whales and seals warm.

Caribou The wild reindeer of North America.

Caterpillar track A loop around the wheels of a tractor or other vehicle that helps it get a good grip on rough ground.

Climate The usual pattern of weather in a particular region.

Cold War The time from the late 1940s to the late 1980s when the United States and the USSR were enemies.

Curling A game in which flat heavy stones are slid over ice toward a target.

Floe A large sheet of floating sea ice.

Glacier A mass of frozen ice that moves slowly down from high ground.

Harpoon A weapon like a spear with a long cord attached to it.

Hydroelectric power Electricity that is generated by using the energy from running water.

Ice cap A mass of ice that permanently covers the land in the polar regions.

Kayak An Inuit canoe for one person.

Komatik An Inuit wooden sled.

Migrate Move from one area to settle in another.

Minerals Substances that are found in the earth and can be mined.

Nomadic Moving from place to place, to hunt or to find food and water.

Nuclear reactor A device that produces nuclear energy, a very powerful form of energy.

Pack ice Ice blocks that form a mass of floating sea ice.

Permafrost Permanently frozen rocks and soil.

Plateau An area of high flatland.

Prefabricated Assembled from parts already made in a factory.

Prospector A person who searches for places where gold or other precious resources can be mined.

Radioactive pollution Pollution caused when dangerous particles produced by nuclear reactions are released into the atmosphere.

Snowmobile A gasoline-driven snow-scooter.

Tundra The treeless frozen plain found in the far north.

Whaling Using ships to hunt whales.

Further Information

Books to read

Alexander, Bryan and Cherry. *Inuit* (Threatened Cultures). Austin, TX: Thomson Learning, 1992.

Bonner, Nigel. *Polar Regions* (Habitats). Austin, TX: Thomson Learning, 1995.

Bullen, Sue. *The Arctic and Its People* (People and Places). Austin, TX: Thomson Learning, 1994.

Markle, Sandra. *Pioneering Frozen Worlds*. New York: Simon and Schuster Children's Group, 1996.

Stonehouse, Bernard. *Snow, Ice, and Cold*. Parsippany, NJ: Silver Burdett, 1992.

Taylor, Barbara. *Arctic and Antarctic* (Eyewitness). New York: Knopf Books for Young Readers, 1995.

Vitebsky, Piers. *Saami of Lapland* (Threatened Cultures). Austin, TX: Thomson Learning, 1993.

Williams, Lawrence. *Polar Lands* (Last Frontiers). Tarrytown, NY: Marshall Cavendish, 1990.

Useful addresses

You can find more information about polar regions, and the people who live in them, if you write to the following organizations:

Earth Living Foundation
P.O. Box 188
Hesperus, CO 81326
(970) 385-5500

Friends of the Earth
1025 Vermont Avenue NW
Suite 300
Washington, D.C. 20005-6303
(202) 783-7400

Greenpeace U.S.A.
1436 U Street, NW
Washington, D.C. 20009

Indigenous Survival International
Suite 300, 47 Clarence Street
Ottawa, Ontario
Canada K1N 9K1

Tungavik Federation of Nunavut
Suite 800, 130 Slater Street
Ottawa, Ontario
Canada K1P 6E2

World Wildlife Fund
1250 24th Street NW
P.O. Box 96555
Washington, D.C. 20077-7795

Picture acknowledgments
The publishers would like to thank the following for allowing their pictures to be used in this book:
Bryan and Cherry Alexander *Cover*, 7, 10, 12, 13, 14 (top), 18, 19 (top), 20, 22/Ann Hawthorne, 24, 25, 26, 27, 28, 29 (top), 30, 32, 33, 35, 36, 38, 44, 45; Bruce Coleman 6/Thomas Buchholz, 29 (lower)/Dr Eckart Pott, 31, 34/Staffan Widstrand, 38, 39/Dr Eckart Pott; Environmental Images 42/Mark Warford; Mary Evans 15, 16; Getty Images *Imprint and Contents pages*/Jean Pragen, *Chapter openers*/David Hisier, 4, 5/Kim Heacox, 9 (lower)/John Edwards, 11/Paul Harris, 14 (lower), 19 (lower)/Natalie Fobes, 37, 40/Alan Levenson, 41/Kathy Bushue, 43/Ben Osborne; Robert Harding 17, 21 (lower)/Dr T. Waltham; NHPA *Title page*/B & C Alexander, 21 (top)/B & C Alexander, 23 /B & C Alexander.
Maps are by Peter Bull.

Index

Page numbers in **bold** refer to photographs.